Small Town
PENNSYLVANIA

Dennis Wolfe

Schiffer
Publishing Ltd

4880 Lower Valley Road • Atglen, PA 19310

Acknowledgments

I would like to thank the following people for their encouragement and support:

Charlotte and Chuck Allwein, Mt. Gretna; Bob and Nancy Bogar, McClure; Linda Covilli, St. Charles, Missouri; Cos Curry, Berwick; Nebbie DiAugustine, Berwick; Amy and Mike Donghia, Linesville; Jon Drager, Jefferson Hills; Joe and Kathleen Herb, Selinsgrove; Jay, John and Sally Hilsher, South Williamsport; Susan Hoyt, Huntington Mills; Logan Hulstine, Middletown; Peggy Hunter, Middletown; Ben Olsen, Washington, DC; Wendy Royal and Marty Wilcox, of *Where and When* magazine, Mt. Joy; Buzz and Polly Savidge, Selinsgrove; Brenda Shultz, Bloomsburg; Ila Stabile and Nadeen Steffey, Canonsburg; and Patricia Wolfe, Cape May, New Jersey

Also, thanks to many, many teachers and professors, whose dedication and knowledge gave me the skills needed to tackle a project like this, and especially to Lois Miller, whose love of American history instilled in me an appreciation of history and heritage, and all things that might otherwise be described as Americana, and to G. Robert Heilman, whose English classes were not just entertaining, to say the least, but were also invaluable in fine tuning and enhancing the appreciation and understanding that I have for language today.

Other Schiffer Books on Related Subjects:
Bucks County Pennsylvania, 978-0-7643-4025-3, $29.99
Chester County Out & About, 978-0-7643-3625-6, $45.00
Lancaster County Out & About, 978-0-7643-3923-3, $29.99

Copyright © 2012 by Dennis Wolfe
All photos © 2012 by Dennis Wolfe

Library of Congress Control Number: 2012945672

Cover and book designed by: Bruce Waters
Type set in Humanist 521

ISBN: 978-0-7643-4176-2
Printed in China

Published by Schiffer Publishing, Ltd.
4880 Lower Valley Road
Atglen, PA 19310
Phone: (610) 593-1777; Fax: (610) 593-2002
E-mail: Info@schifferbooks.com

For the largest selection of fine reference books on this and related subjects, please visit our website at:
www.schifferbooks.com.
You may also write for a free catalog.

This book may be purchased from the publisher.
Please try your bookstore first.

We are always looking for people to write books on new and related subjects. If you have an idea for a book, please contact us at:
proposals@schifferbooks.com

Schiffer Books are available at special discounts for bulk purchases for sales promotions or premiums. Special editions, including personalized covers, corporate imprints, and excerpts can be created in large quantities for special needs. For more information contact the publisher.

In Europe, Schiffer books are distributed by
Bushwood Books
6 Marksbury Ave.
Kew Gardens
Surrey TW9 4JF England
Phone: 44 (0) 20 8392 8585; Fax: 44 (0) 20 8392 9876
E-mail: info@bushwoodbooks.co.uk
Website: www.bushwoodbooks.co.uk

Foreword

So many places, and, as it turns out, so little time. Pennsylvania has a wealth of history, scenery, and culture. This book attempts to recognize those many and varied attractions, focusing on small towns, generally having populations less than 10,000, and also, with some exceptions, places that aren't in a metropolitan area.

Working on this over the course of several years, I've tried to represent all parts of the state as fairly as possible, but surely there will be some readers who will lament the lack of coverage of this parade, or that festival, and they will probably be correct. Weather, other commitments, and numerous other difficulties made it impossible to be everywhere, although I certainly tried!

So what is this book about? The generous reader will conclude that it's a wonderfully eclectic collection of scenes and events from all corners of the state. (Since I generally don't hear anyone other than politicians and state employees refer to Pennsylvania as "The Commonwealth," I'll use the more generic term "state" in general usage.) Others may conclude that it's an incoherent mess, with no apparent theme. To me, it's about landscapes, streetscapes, old buildings, new buildings, trees, shrubs, flowers, ponds, lakes, rivers, and people just enjoying what Pennsylvania has to offer. If I can get the reader to say "Wow!" or "I didn't know that!" or "I'd like to see that!", then I have succeeded.

I chose to write this in first-person conversational, because I have much experience in putting people to sleep with past slide shows. You can go at your own pace, however, on this one. Take your time, enjoy the pictures, and then go out and see something you discovered on these pages!

KEYSTONE ROAD TRIP

A Photographic Journey through Small Town PA

We can agree that Greene County is in Southwestern Pennsylvania, just as Wayne County is certainly part of Northeastern Pennsylvania, but where, exactly, is the dividing line between Central and Western Pennsylvania, or Central and Eastern? Northern and Southern? Different publications seem to have different answers to that question. For that reason, this "road trip," which is really the combination of dozens of such trips, will begin in Greene County, and take one continuous route, winding its way north to Erie County, then across the Northern Tier, then through the counties along or near the Delaware River, and finally, following a rather tortuous, serpentine path through the counties of the center of the state, just so I can end it at my home base of Snyder County!

Greene County

Drive west, you're in West Virginia. Drive south, you're in West Virginia. We begin our journey in Greene County, at the I-79 Welcome Center, and we're going to be heading east and then north.

A miner's memorial inside the Welcome Center. Without question, this facility is a Pennsylvania promoter.

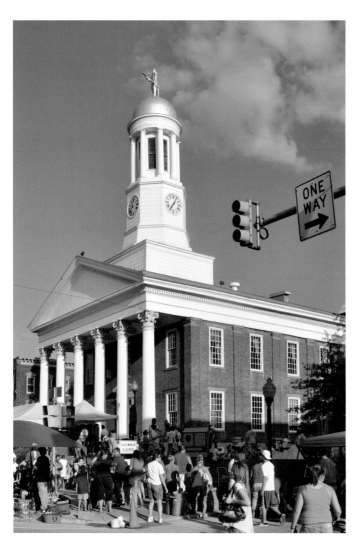

THE WELCOME CENTER on I-79, north of the West Virginia state line. It's July 29th, "Rain Day," in Waynesburg, where it allegedly rains most years, but on this day there's only brilliant sunshine!

THE COX FARM BRIDGE, north of Waynesburg, was built in the 1940s. At only about thirty-two feet long, it isn't even the shortest one in Greene County.

Fayette County

Any visitor to Fayette County will be quickly aware of the region's association to the French and Indian War, and the Marquis de la Fayette, for whom the county was named. Uniontown, Connellsville, the Nemacolin Woodlands Resort, Fort Necessity Battlefield, Braddock's Grave, and Ohiopyle State Park are all in Fayette County.

A February morning provides this frosty scene near the FAYETTE COUNTY COURTHOUSE.

Uniontown native George C. Marshall, who formulated the Marshall Plan to help rebuild post-World War II Europe, is honored in this plaza at the western end of the city.

Uniontown's renewal, dubbed "Marshall Plan II," is acknowledged in this mural.

Around twenty feet high, this is one of many such statues found around the country. They began in the early 1960s as Paul Bunyan statues, morphed into "Muffler Men," and have been used in many other incarnations as well. You will see a similar one in Kittanning.

Somerset County

Called the "Roof Garden of Pennsylvania," Somerset County has the highest average elevation of any county in Pennsylvania, as well as Mt. Davis, the highest point in the state. There will be snow in this county when there is snow in few other places. Seven Springs and Hidden Valley, both year-round resorts, are among the first ski areas to open and among the last to close for the season.

Lizzy, Luke, Leroy, and Lexie, residents of Scullton, pose for the camera...and then walk away when they realize that the photographer isn't offering them any food.

The **SOMERSET COUNTY COURTHOUSE** commands a dominant presence over downtown Somerset.

When they first appeared in Somerset County, close to the Pennsylvania Turnpike, wind turbines were a novelty. Now, of course, they're everywhere.

7

MOUNTAIN VIEW FARM, in Roxbury, presents a colorful picture for travelers on PA 31.

The permanent memorial to the passengers of Flight 93, who died in the terrorist attacks of September 11, 2001, is to be located in a field in Somerset County, but was not quite finished at the time of this book's publication. The temporary memorial included an outpouring of sentiment and support from visitors worldwide.

As people sit by the pool and sip on their lattés, they should never forget the blood, sweat, and tears of those who came before us and made it possible for many today to have a better life than they did. This marker in Windber commemorates their sacrifices.

Cambria County

Industrial, rural, high elevation, low elevation, new, old — these are all words that can describe Cambria County, a word derived from the Latin for "Wales."

BELOW: Due to continuous efforts by the borough to prevent Dutch Elm disease, Westmont's Luzerne Street has the longest continuous stretch of American Elms left in the country. ABOVE: This is what the fuss is about — Elms produce a leafy canopy that is rivaled by only a few other species of trees.

The remains of more than seven hundred unidentified victims of the 1889 Johnstown flood rest here in **GRANDVIEW CEMETERY**, in the borough of Southmont.

It's the world's steepest inclined plane railway and you can even take your car with you.

Said to be the largest free-flying U.S. flag in the country, this one stands above the Johnstown Incline.

Even though the highest point in Pennsylvania is lower than the highest point in most other states in the Appalachians, anyone familiar with the Laurel Highlands knows that even at the elevation here on PA 271, near the boundaries of Somerset, Cambria, and Westmoreland counties, the winter weather can be dramatically different than in nearby lower-lying Johnstown.

Indiana County

Known as the Christmas Tree Capital of the World, Indiana County is mostly rural, and the Borough of Indiana is clearly this county's nerve center.

At the confluence of Loyalhanna Creek and the Conemaugh River, Saltsburg was a canal town whose past is well preserved and respected in this Indiana County community.

The statue of Jimmy Stewart in front of the **INDIANA COUNTY COURTHOUSE** captures the actor as a man of honor and virtue.

Westmoreland County

Take a good look at a map of Westmoreland County. It's all over the place! Towns you didn't think were in Westmoreland County *are in* Westmoreland County! This fact alone makes it difficult to describe, so I will let the pictures do the talking.

VANDERGRIFT was a planned worker's community, with innovative buildings, such as this one, dotting the town's landscape.

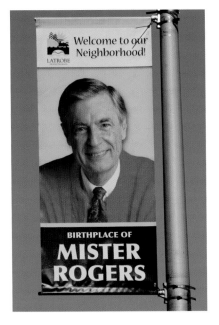

Latrobe was home to both Mister Rogers and Arnold Palmer.

ST. VINCENT COLLEGE in Latrobe.

One of the original Lincoln Highway markers, now in a slightly different location in Ligonier.

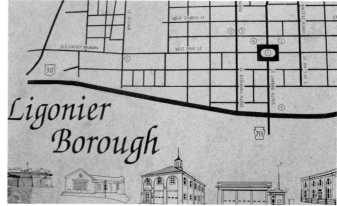

This is a clever idea. It isn't on a wall... It's on the sidewalk.

As in many small towns, summer in Ligonier is a time for evening concerts.

Allegheny County

South Hills, North Hills, meaning south and north of Pittsburgh — everything relates to the industrial, but also cultural giant, Pittsburgh. As I noted earlier, I did not focus on places in metropolitan areas, only because that allowed me to give more attention to lesser-known areas. However, I can tell you this about Allegheny County and Pittsburgh: If ever you decide that you're going to take a vacation there, don't let anyone laugh about that, because if they do, that will be an indication that they're not really familiar with the city or the region.

The more you look at the ornamentation on the exterior of the **OAKMONT POST OFFICE**, the more you appreciate it.

This isn't just an original way to separate the sidewalk from the street; the choice of colors here in Carnegie, Allegheny County, is intriguing.

I'll stipulate that Pittsburgh isn't a town with fewer than 10,000 people, despite decades of population loss, but the nationality rooms at the University of Pittsburgh represent the heritage of ethnic groups that can be found all over Pennsylvania. Each of these rooms, around thirty of them, is routinely used as a regular classroom, and is a genuine art treasure. If these rooms, located mostly around the perimeter of the ground floor of the Cathedral of Learning, would be the only things you saw on a trip to Pittsburgh, they alone would justify the visit.

The Italian Room

The Polish Room

The German Room

(Nationality Room Pictures used with permission from the University of Pittsburgh)

Washington County

Like every county in the Pittsburgh Region, Washington County is a mix of old and new, industrial and rural. With Ohio to its west and Pittsburgh to the northeast, it seems that the county is almost separated from most of the rest of Pennsylvania. It would probably amuse folks there to know that many of the good people in the more eastern counties know very little about it. (Hence, this book!)

There's just something about this paint job in West Brownsville, Washington County. Brownsville lies across the river in Fayette County.

Here at Speers, just south of Charleroi, the Monongahela is a river of both recreation and commerce.

Canonsburg boasts the largest July 4th parade in
Pennsylvania outside of Philadelphia.

In my humble opinion, the California University campus has developed
into one of the most striking in the state university system.

The twelve-foot-high statue of Vulcan, Roman god
of fire and volcanoes, also the University mascot, is a
recent addition to the California campus.

The Mon Valley Leathernecks from World War II represent a brave group whose numbers are dwindling.

Canonsburg is a lively town. One of its numerous special celebrations is Oktoberfest.

Jon Drager, Dan Hartman, and Zach DeCicco, all of Jefferson Hills, in Allegheny County, got my attention when Dan shouted out: "Photo op, right here." We got to talking a bit, and it turns out that these very personable guys were graduates of Thomas Jefferson High School. Zach, as it turns out, quarterbacked the 2007 TJ team to one of its three state football championships.

Bobby Vinton and this other well-known gentleman, Perry Como, are natives of Canonsburg.

This building, just outside Canonsburg, says "ice cream" all over it!

Beaver County

Beaver, Beaver Falls, Big Beaver. Enough! I get it! Actually, Beaver County is another of those industrial/rural, old/new counties, and still has a very important industrial base, but also a wealth of rural beauty.

Kara Reffett's radiant smile welcomes you to the **Sts. Peter and Paul Ukrainian Catholic Church** stand at Nationality Days in Ambridge, Beaver County.

The word game, displayed here for Nationality Days, comes in Russian as well!

This might be one of the few "themed" school buildings anywhere. In Ambridge, if you build a school with a bridge motif, then comes a real bridge to the main entrance!

The renovated **BUCHANAN BUILDING** in Beaver is a visual feast.

Downtown Beaver, with its wide main street, is one of the most physically appealing county seats in Pennsylvania.

Signs, like this one in Rochester, can be found in all of Beaver County's river towns. (As you might have guessed.)

A replica of a former courthouse accents a major intersection in downtown Beaver.

As this scene illustrates, the industrial heritage of Beaver County's river towns is never very far away.

Spend any time in Beaver Falls, and you'll be aware of hometown boy Joe Namath, well-known former football star in the NFL.

Glass block can be very interesting. Cobalt blue glass block, like this example in New Brighton, is *really* interesting!

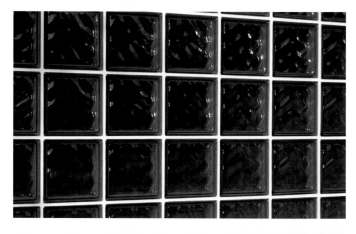

Lawrence County

New Castle is the Fireworks Capital of America and Evans City was part of the location filming of the gruesome (but fun) cult classic *Night of the Living Dead*. However, my favorite has to be SNPJ, and I mean that as a positive. SNPJ stands for "Slovenska Narodna Podpoma Jednota."

Yes, that's its name!

More places should have signs like this one in Ellwood City.

The well-manicured campus of **WESTMINSTER COLLEGE** in New Wilmington. I always seem to manage to visit these places when there is no one around!

Butler County

In Zelienople, Saxonburg, New Year's Eve celebrations take place at 6:00 p.m. because that's when it's midnight in Germany… Something suggests some strong German influences in this county. It's more than that, though. The county seat of the same name is the birthplace of the Jeep — and we can't forget that Mars is here, too!

One of many fine buildings in a concentrated area of Harmony, Butler County.

It isn't just another New Year's Eve Celebration. This one is at 6:00 p.m. Eastern Standard Time, on December 31st, because, as noted above, at that time, it's midnight in Germany!

ZANELLA MILLING, in West Sunbury, still has the charm of an old-time feed and general supply store.

Right here in Saxonburg is a replica of the Brooklyn Bridge. The bridge's designer, John Augustus Roebling, was a one-time resident of Saxonburg.

Slippery Rock claims to be the town known round the world. I don't doubt it for a minute. I once attended a football game between Cal-Berkeley and Stanford, at Stanford. Near the end of the game, the PA announcer intoned somberly, in words reasonably close to these, "Ladies and Gentlemen, this score just in from the east: Slippery Rock 21, Susquehanna 7." Why am I retelling this? He made it up! As a Susquehanna graduate and a resident of the Selinsgrove area, I knew that no such game had been played. Apparently, saying those odd sounding words was his idea of great fun! Slippery Rock is, indeed, known far and wide.

Well, this is Mars! What did you expect?

The **NORTH COUNTRY BREWING COMPANY** is a landmark in downtown Slippery Rock.

Armstrong County

Kittanning and Ford City, just downriver, form the heart and soul of Armstrong County, but the county also has the distinction of having the smallest "city" in the state. I put that word in quotes, because the city, Parker, has a population of less than 1,000, but it is incorporated as a city. It might also be the only city other than Philadelphia that is in one county and is bordered by two others: Butler to the west and Clarion to the east.

Brady Wegener is amazing! Billing himself as "The Class Clown," this young man, shown here in Kittanning as he juggles while on stilts, is not only an acrobat, but a master showman as well.

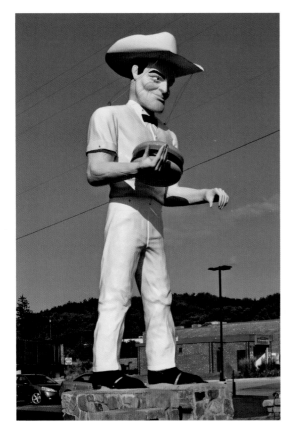

As referred to earlier, here's another "Muffler Man" at a restaurant east of Kittanning.

The shoreline of **KITTANNING'S ALLEGHENY RIVER** has been beautifully developed over the past few years.

Jefferson County

Brookville and Brockway... they're up there in the northern part of Jefferson County, but, like it or not, the star is down south — and its name is Punxsutawney. Who knew that groundhogs could ever become so popular?

It's a sleepy Sunday afternoon in downtown Brookville.

And there may well be Eagles here...

...but this is definitely Steelers Country!

There are more than thirty of these critters in and around Punxsutawney (aka Punxsy) and some of them are real! This one is either tending to the garden or fixing the lawn mower.

Forest County

There are no traffic lights here, except for the one at the local museum, but there is the beautiful Allegheny River — and woods. Lots and lots of woods… Forest County could be the definition of serenity.

The Allegheny River sparkles in the background while a butterfly feasts on this Teasel plant (*Dipsacus sylvestris*, for those who were asking) in Tionesta.

This unlikely structure is in Tionesta, overlooking a section of the Allegheny River that isn't navigable. Just a few years old, it was built by a Tionesta resident whose interest in lighthouses led him to construct it as a gift to the town and to honor his family. It's a real surprise on first sight.

Clarion County

It's very rural, but Clarion, the home of Clarion University, is the pulse of this county. The county is also home to part of the outstanding Cook Forest State Park.

You'll find a collection of monuments in downtown Clarion that is surpassed by very few other places.

The Seneca Valley High School band, from Butler County, marches in the Fall Foliage parade in downtown Clarion.

Venango County

Oil City. Franklin. Drake Oil Well. A top-notch rail trail. Some first-rate festivals and cottages along the Allegheny. This star of northwestern Pennsylvania is a fascinating region for both its charm and history.

The **DeBence Antique Music World**, at 1261 Liberty Street, Franklin, is a one-of-a-kind museum. Even if you didn't think you were interested in something like this, you were probably wrong!

Liberty Street in Franklin is the scene for most of Franklin's special events. The **Venango County Courthouse** is situated prominently on a bend in the street.

February is ice-carving time in downtown Franklin.

This is the only way to eat an apple pie if you're in a contest!

These are two of several sculptures to be found along the banks of Oil Creek and the Allegheny River in Oil City.

Mercer County

Depending on where you are in Mercer County, you might experience radical changes in scenery from one mile to the next. From the industrial dynamos of Sharon and Farrell, and the western terminus of Pennsylvania's section of Interstate 80, to the tranquility of Goddard State Park, Mercer is truly diverse.

AVENUE OF FLAGS. The avenue of 444 flags (actually East State Street) in Hermitage, Mercer County, was built to honor the American hostages who were held for 444 days by the Iranian government from 1979 to 1981.

The imposing **MERCER COUNTY COURTHOUSE** is one of the few in Pennsylvania that is situated in a central square, dominating the downtown Mercer landscape.

That little red line on the floor is the attraction here, especially to someone like me, having lived most of my life in an area that is around ninety miles from the nearest state line. At the **PENN-OHIO DELI AND LOTTERY** in Sharon, that red line separates Ohio, on the right, from Pennsylvania. Want an Ohio lottery ticket? Step right up — to the counter on the right, that is. If you want a Pennsylvania lottery ticket, you'll have to go to the opposite end of the counter. Well, you can't buy Pennsylvania lottery tickets in Ohio!

SLOVAK FOLK CRAFTS, just west of Grove City, is a treasure trove of art and collectibles from Slovakia and other places around the world.

Grove City's downtown is alive with historical reminders, including this recent addition to the side of the **GUTHRIE THEATER**.

Just a part of the beautiful **GROVE CITY COLLEGE CAMPUS**.

Crawford County

With Pennsylvania's largest natural lake, plus a man-made one shared with Ohio, water is never far away — at least not in western Crawford County. The eastern end of the county also includes Titusville, which is famous for a very different reason.

The southern shore of Conneaut Lake, Pennsylvania's largest natural lake.

The *Kaylee Belle* traverses the waters of the lake.

Smashing pumpkins is great fun at Conneaut Lake Park, but either the pumpkin or the school bus should perhaps be a different color. Of course, watching it fall was the best part, so who cares about color!

A cooperative effort between Allegheny College and PennDOT has produced this colorful and innovative wall of recycled signs, right along US 6, just west of Meadville. The wall, about two-tenths of a mile long, has garnered national attention for its unique contribution to roadside art.

Downtown Titusville is the site of not only the **BLUE CANOE**, but this mural, which nicely commemorates the city's history. Site of the world's first commercial oil well, just a few miles from downtown, in Venango County, Titusville's history is among the most important in northwestern Pennsylvania.

Titusville was home to John Heisman, one of the early innovators in the game of football.

The **OIL CREEK AND TITUSVILLE RAILROAD**, based in Titusville, now takes train and history buffs through the Oil Creek valley.

At the Linesville spillway, the fish will literally jump out of the water to get a bite from humans eager to please.

Sunset over Ohio? This is the view of Pymatuning Lake from Espyville — and it is indeed the state of Ohio on the opposite shore.

Erie County

If you turn on the radio on a hot summer day and hear that the temperature may reach the high 30s, you just might be in Erie County, because you're listening to a Canadian radio station. If you go to see a hockey game at the Tullio Arena in downtown Erie, you're likely to hear "O Canada" at the beginning of the game, because the semi-pro Erie Otters are members of the Ontario Hockey League. Such is life in Erie County, which is closer to Buffalo and Cleveland and, in a straight line at least, to London, Ontario, than it is to Pittsburgh.

In northwestern Pennsylvania, there are no diners, just "dinors."

A barn with a picture of a barn, near Union City, Erie County.

This is Rosé Ribbett, a transplant from Erie, when that city had an art project involving stylized frogs decorated in various ways. She now resides in North East.

A very impressive building for a branch campus. Once a seminary, this is now part of **MERCYHURST COLLEGE**.

Grapes, and then some more grapes, are one of the prominent crops in Erie County.

In North East, you'll see brave souls volunteer to stomp grapes at the annual Winefest in September.

Even this downtown alley is into the grape theme.

The sunsets over Lake Erie are as dramatic as any you'll see on the ocean.

This handsome college town in southern Erie County boasts its own lake, plus another on the campus of Edinboro University.

Even on a weeknight, this lakeside restaurant in Edinboro is crowded.

Warren County

You know you're in someplace special when you see Warren. A beautiful setting and grand old streets mark this city as a place with a history. Elsewhere in the county is the Kinzua Dam, the highest dam in the state, built primarily for flood control, but also creating the huge Allegheny Reservoir. Although building it involved breaking a treaty signed by President George Washington, there is no question that its presence has been instrumental in preventing both flooding and drought.

In the course of this book, you'll see more sunsets than sunrises, not because they're easier, but because I'm not one of those morning people I keep hearing about. This sunrise, taken one February morning in Warren, was particularly invigorating since it was about 10 degrees below zero.

The upper Allegheny complements downtown Warren.

The flags of France, England, the United States, and the city of Warren fly over the city.

One of Warren's most impressive assets is the sheer number of fine old Victorian era buildings that line the streets near the courthouse.

Recent renovations have given downtown Warren an entirely new look.

Nearby **CHAPMAN STATE PARK** is the site of Winterfest.

An oil refinery is just part of Warren's varied landscape.

I didn't make the sign, I just photographed it!

Outside of some of the state's larger cities, this is one of the most impressive fountains to be found anywhere in the state.

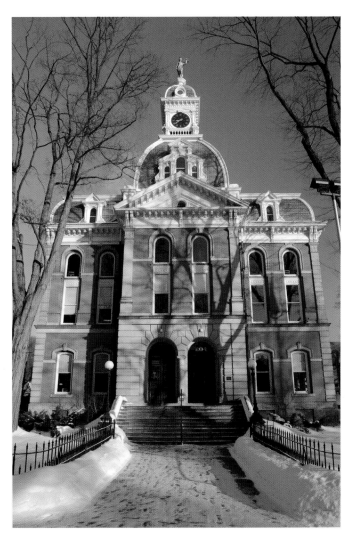

On an otherwise gloomy and overcast day, the sun peeked out just before it set, here at **WOLF POINT MARINA**, near Kinzua dam.

One of my favorite courthouses. Remember this building when we get to Elk County.

McKean County

To an outsider like myself, McKean County is just fascinating from one end to the other: Bradford, hard by the New York state line; Kane, way down at the other end; and the partially destroyed Kinzua Bridge, once a great place to spit from...just to see how long it took for it to reach Kinzua Creek. If it's any consolation, I did think about whether or not I wanted to include that last sentence, but you know people did it! The center supports were destroyed by a tornado in 2003, but DCNR has constructed a viewing area at the end of the bridge.

World renowned Zippo® is a proud part of the city of Bradford.

Stunning. I will use that word in only one other place in this book. Four stories high, but only twenty-two feet wide, the **OPTION HOUSE** is so named because of what once transpired here. Built in 1902, it was the meeting place for holders of oil options who would sit and discuss what each other had to offer, hence the name of the building. The structure is a destination in itself, it is that outstanding.

Bradford is a cold spot in Pennsylvania, and actually "lost" a contest, to Fargo, North Dakota, for the country's worst weather. So it snows! Philadelphia had snowfalls like this, too!

A working oil well sits at the rear of a well-known fast-food chain in downtown Bradford.

It isn't all about oil! Just ask Olivia and Serena, of the Bradford area, who have been successfully selling lemonade for several years!

As part of an effort to promote US Route 6, this huge mural was painted on the side of a building in Mt. Jewett. If you're headed west, you'll miss it if you don't know it's there.

Situated in another part of McKean County is Kane, "Black Cherry Capital of the World." Twenty-five miles or so from any other town of real size, Kane is a jewel in the wilderness.

Another great town along US Route 6 is Smethport, the home of the inventor of "Wooly Willy."
(If you don't know what that is, you won't care.) Hamlin Lake is one of Smethport's big attractions.

The area's lumber industry made some wealthy, and that wealth led to the
construction of many remarkable mansions, like this one.

Tucked away in northern McKean County, near the New York State line, is Eldred, which, during World War II, was the site of a munitions plant that is now a first-class museum dedicated to depicting that war.

Elk County

You *will* find elk in Elk County, and you might not even have to be that patient. Areas around the village of Benezette, as well as nearby Winslow Hill, usually will reward you with some sightings, but, if not, they are almost sure to turn up somewhere around sunrise. This wild and wonderful county also includes Johnsonburg, site of an active paper mill.

The recently opened **ELK COUNTRY VISITOR'S CENTER**, near Benezette, is an absolutely first-class facility that helps visitors to the region understand more about the elk population, its habits, and its effect on the surroundings.

I suppose if you get accustomed to it, it's no big deal having elk grazing in your backyard. That's exactly what residents of some parts of Elk County, especially around Benezette, can expect on a routine basis. Some of the elk, like these two, are fairly tame; others are as skittish as deer.

If the **ELK COUNTY COURTHOUSE** in Ridgway looks familiar, that's because it's based on the same plans as the Warren County Courthouse. What better way to spend a Friday evening in the summer than to watch the world go by from right here?

Another perspective on the building, but this time it's cold outside!

The **ELK COUNTRY STORE** in Medix Run provides a warm respite from a cold winter day.

TWO SCOOPS, an old-time ice cream parlor, is right across the street from the courthouse.

Think wood — carved wood — and lots of it. Ridgway is home to the **Chainsaw Carving Rendezvous** in February. Evidence of that annual event is everywhere... There's one on the roof.

Here's another one at the actual rendezvous.

This one was added to the downtown scene a few years ago.

And here are more from the rendezvous... This really is a world class event.

To the east of Ridgway is St. Marys, which is really just a small town that absorbed a surrounding township and incorporated as a city, becoming, in the process, one of Pennsylvania's largest in land area.

An eternal flame marks this veteran's memorial in downtown St. Marys.

Cameron County

If it seems like I've already used the word "woods" too often, I haven't. Woods! Cameron County is mostly woods and very little else. Sinnemahoning Creek and its various branches take up almost all of Cameron County, which, like its northern neighbor, could easily be dubbed "God's Country."

Sometimes there's an attraction in the simplest of objects. These little fish bowls at a street fair in Emporium did it for me!

Small but tranquil, Emporium is the county seat of Cameron County. In this picture, PA 120 heads west towards St. Marys.

Potter County

Three different major North American watersheds — the Great Lakes, the Mississippi, and the Chesapeake Bay — all have sources in Potter County, where streams flow north, south, east, and west. As noted before, Potter County calls itself "God's Country," and it truly is a hunting and fishing paradise. However, it's also a place where the quality of life can be outstanding.

The Eagle stands guard at the Coudersport borough building.

Here's a well known river that's just getting its start in life. This is none other than the Allegheny River, flowing south through Coudersport. It's still just a relative trickle.

This fantastic interior is just a part of **OLGA'S GALLERY, CAFÉ, AND BISTRO** in downtown Coudersport.

Olga, from Ukraine, is also an expert in making decorative eggs.

Downtown Coudersport looks like it was frozen in time from the 1880s, and I mean that in every good way.

Denton Hill ski area has a lodge that allows you to enjoy the outside from the warmth of the inside.

At the eastern end of Potter County is Galeton, a small town that takes advantage of its setting along Pine Creek.

Tioga County

No doubt about it, the stars of this county are, well, everywhere. Mansfield, Wellsboro, and the "Pennsylvania Grand Canyon" do not exhaust the list. Visitors come from all over the world to see the sights in this Northern Tier jewel.

Looking west down Main Street in Wellsboro.

Idyllic Wellsboro is special for residents and visitors alike. It's all about gas lights, apparently, and there's no doubt they do add something unique to the town. Pictured here is "The Green," which is a great open space that encompasses numerous monuments.

Larry Biddison and David Davies do their part to make a Dickens Christmas a success in downtown Wellsboro.

The warm and inviting **PENN WELLS HOTEL** is one of Wellsboro's treasures. Note the Christmas ball flag on the wall.

Another Wellsboro landmark is the **WELLSBORO DINER** (we're not in northwestern Pennsylvania anymore, so diner is spelled with an "e"). I can attest to the fact that the food in both the hotel and the diner is excellent.

This picture is the result of one of those happy accidents. By taking the wrong road out of town, I came upon this icy but photogenic scene!

When I first saw this gentleman standing on the green, reading that newspaper, I thought he was unusually still. I actually had to get closer to realize that it was a sculpture.

On my next visit to Wellsboro, he had moved down the street to this location. Now he's gone completely. I could easily have found out what happened to him, but some things are better off as an enduring mystery.

One of the prominent buildings on the campus of **MANSFIELD UNIVERSITY**.

Meanwhile, in Morris, another part of Tioga County, the Morris rattlesnake roundup succeeds in getting an accurate assessment of the rattlers' well being in these parts.

Bradford County

Something is up in Bradford County. A notable number of barns, and sometimes other buildings, are displaying these designs. It turns out that the Wyalusing Chamber of Commerce is encouraging area residents to display original designs, called barn quilts. As the following images show, the response has been very positive.

This one is in New Albany

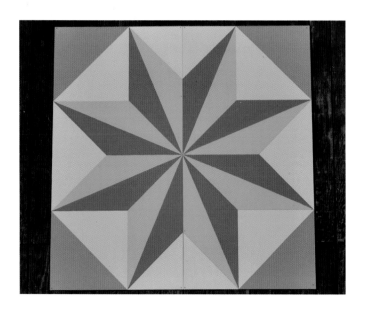

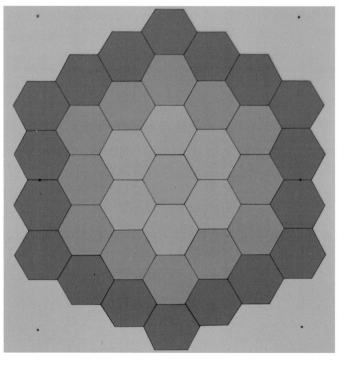

It isn't without controversy. Drilling for natural gas, in a geologic formation called the Marcellus Shale, has changed the commercial environment in Bradford County and elsewhere in the state. The drilling rigs come and go. Many operate 24 hours a day. This one, set up near Wysox, is typical of those found in Bradford and neighboring counties. At a distance, the sound produced by one of these operations becomes a continuous hum, which, in the still air of a summer night, is almost hypnotic.

Towanda, like other Route 6 communities, has a wealth of grand old buildings.

MERRILL PARKWAY parallels the Susquehanna River.

Right place, right time. These guys were having a grand old time as participants in an amateur video. Without warning, they came running down the street and I happened to catch this action. Now, I think I'm on YouTube.

Another shot of downtown Towanda, this time looking south, and with no fuchsia, or whatever it is, in the background.

A bit chilly on this autumn day, but a nice gathering place in downtown Athens.

Saving an old school bell in Sayre.

Sayre has streets and homes that would be perfect as movie locations.

Another scenic spot in Sayre.

If you have never seen the view from Wyalusing rocks, I could say this was a sunrise, but, no, it's another sunset on the Susquehanna.

Susquehanna County

Not only is Susquehanna County closer to New York than to most of Pennsylvania, much of it is part of the greater Binghamton area. It's also where you'll find the Susquehanna River in its first voyage into the state, before it heads back to New York. Montrose, the county seat, could pass for a small town right out of Connecticut or Vermont.

Although New Milford is some distance away from Wyalusing, Lynn-Lee is a participant in the barn quilt project.

The **LYNN-LEE BED AND BREAKFAST** in New Milford is an inviting place to be any season of the year.

ST. MARK'S EPISCOPAL CHURCH in New Milford has a New England look to it.

I'm into these retro style restaurants, but this is in a private residence in Hallstead! As you can see, the owners have taken great pride in their attention to detail. I really do love these places.

If you're looking for an old-time country store, find one that *says* it's an old-time country store, like this one in Hop Bottom.

In the Susquehanna county seat of Montrose, an old-time fire station.

Blueberries are the main attraction in this August event in Montrose, but I don't think that's what these siblings are discussing.

A gazebo with a somewhat different look.

Wyoming County

The still mostly pristine Susquehanna winds its way down through Wyoming County, where it passes through Tunkhannock, one of the most beautiful small towns in Pennsylvania. In the northeastern part of the county is the wondrous Tunkhannock Viaduct.

The cupola on the **WYOMING COUNTY COURTHOUSE** is typical of northern Pennsylvania architecture.

The **TUNKHANNOCK VIADUCT**, in Nicholson, never fails to impress me. This is pretty much the standard shot of this structure, taken from an observation area, but it shows how massive it is. Built by the Lackawanna Railroad, it was completed in 1915, and is still in use today. One of the more amazing facts about it is that, coming from either the north or south on US 11, you don't see it until you're almost upon it.

One of Tunkhannock's many venerable and outstanding old homes.

Luzerne County

Luzerne County is dominated by Wilkes-Barre and the Wyoming Valley, but it also includes such star attractions as Harveys Lake, Lake Silkworth, and Ricketts Glen State Park — the site of more waterfalls than any one state park should have a right to!

What better way to enjoy a summer evening than sitting on your deck, if you're lucky enough to have one, at Harveys Lake in Luzerne County.

Pierogies are another of the attractions at the Kielbassa (spelling?) Festival in Plymouth. According to a Google search, it's the **Kielbasa Festival**, but the question is a dig, because it seems there are as many ways of spelling some of these words as there are places that sell them!

White Haven, Luzerne County.
Cold winter night. Pizza! It's no longer Carmine's, but the pizza is still there!

Lackawanna County

As Wilkes-Barre is to Luzerne County, Scranton is to Lackawanna County. Coal mining was the engine that drove the local economy for many years, but is now, of course, less dominant. Also, as with Luzerne County, there is much more to Lackawanna County. The southernmost part of the county, for example, is nearly unpopulated.

The art associated with many Byzantine and Orthodox churches, like this mosaic in Olyphant, is sometimes beyond adequate words.

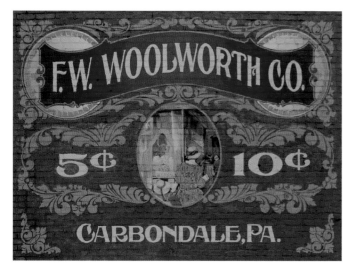

WOOLWORTH'S lives on in Carbondale.

Old Forge means pizza and, even though "Old Forge Style" pizza describes something specific, here is James Sachetti, owner of SACHETTI'S PIZZA, flipping one the old-fashioned way. I would recommend his pizza to anyone!

Pumpkins in Mt. Cobb, Lackawanna County.

Wayne County

Occupying the northeastern corner of Pennsylvania, Wayne County is about fifty miles from north to south. The Wayne Highlands School District, in Honesdale, has found it to be more efficient to allow high school students in the northern end of the county to attend school in Hancock, New York! Here's a piece of trivia that may give new meaning to the concept of trivia: The northeastern corner of Wayne County is less than ninety miles from the southwestern corner of Massachusetts! As for Honesdale, it's a town with enough attractions worthy of a community much larger.

For a town its size, Honesdale has a sizeable downtown business district.

Just off downtown Honesdale is this serene winter view near the courthouse.

One of the cars on the tourist train, named after the president of the Pennsylvania Coal Company.

I suppose I could have put these letters back together, but why spoil the apparently immense fun someone had in separating them on this sign in Hamlin?

The borough of Hawley is east of Honesdale, along US 6.

Pike County

Called the "Birthplace of the American Conservation Movement" and home to two-time governor Gifford Pinchot, the first head of the US Forest Service and an ardent conservationist, Pike County has also experienced an exponential increase in its population. Its proximity to New York City and a more relaxed and less expensive environment has made the county very desirable for those looking for a better life.

On a beautiful winter day at **Promised Land State Park**, Alanna Kieffer, of Lords Valley, pretends that it isn't cold out while sitting for a photo shoot.

Waterfall Country

If you're anywhere near Milford, you're also near at least half a dozen major waterfalls. This is **Shohola Falls**, west on US 6.

DINGMANS FALLS, part of Delaware Water Gap National Recreation Area, south on US 209.

FULMER FALLS, now part of the Delaware Water Gap NRA.

SILVERTHREAD FALLS, near Dingmans Falls.

RAYMONDSKILL FALLS, also part of the Delaware Water Gap NRA.

Downtown Milford is one of the "coolest" small towns in America, according to *Budget Travel*.

Although the county was named for Zebulon Pike, this is definitely a fish, and it might be a pike!

It's cold, but much "stuff" awaits inside.

Connecting Lackawaxen with New York State, this bridge over the Delaware River
is one of the earliest of the Roebling suspension bridges, used at one time as an
aqueduct. Before it was restored, the suspension cables were clearly visible.

A human toll-taker at the historic **DINGMAN'S FERRY BRIDGE**. How many other
places do you figure you'll see that?

Monroe County

A casual passerby might not quite get what the Pocono region is all about, and that's one of its secrets. One has to look beyond the Interstates, and even the very busy US 209, to see that Monroe County and all of the Poconos are full of attractions that aren't "in your face." If you stop and take some time, there's a new surprise almost around every bend in the road.

Vibrant downtown Stroudsburg, the Monroe County seat, is the heart of the Poconos.

At Christmas time, Stroudsburg has an old-time Christmas feel.

In front of the Monroe County Courthouse for a time, the "fish" is now gone!

The **SHERMAN THEATER** survives as a performing arts venue.

An unexpected oasis of tranquility, the **B'NAI HARIM TEMPLE** sits just off PA 940 in Pocono Pines.

Carbon County

Carbon County's very name suggests coal mining, but, except in the Lansford/Nesquehoning area, you won't see widespread evidence of mining here, as you will in neighboring counties. Continuing on US 209, you come to the tourist Mecca of Jim Thorpe and then find still more character to the county as you go on to Lehighton, then Weissport, and Palmerton.

I regret that I was unable to attend this event in Weissport, Carbon County, so you'll have to use your imagination and fill in the blanks.

An abrupt change from the previous picture! The icon screen at **ST. JOHN THE BAPTIST BYZANTINE CATHOLIC CHURCH** in Lansford is stunning! The only other time I used that word in this book was when I was gushing (pun intended) about the Option House in Bradford.

You gotta love the attitude!

These murals are found on a building in Lansford called THE PALACE.
Among those who performed here were the world-famous Dorsey
Brothers, who were from nearby Shenandoah.

The unique design of this fountain in Lehighton is a downtown landmark.

Here's the short version: Jim Thorpe, the man, never visited Jim Thorpe, the town, as far as anyone knows. When he died, his widow didn't feel that his native Oklahoma planned to provide a suitable memorial to him, so she agreed to have him interred in the town that would change its name to honor him. Mauch Chunk and East Mauch Chunk did just that and, ironically, the town that has so much going for it now, probably would be an important tourist destination, even if it were still called Mauch Chunk and East Mauch Chunk.

This view of Jim Thorpe from Flagstaff Mountain justifies the use of the word "nestled."

A very interesting coffee shop on Broadway, downtown's main street, a street that is anything but "broad."

Bill Krieger, a teacher at Shenandoah Valley High School, has painstakingly worked on this mural at **STRANGE BREW** to perfection, and it's now just about complete.

Another tourist railroad... It is just one of many Jim Thorpe attractions.

This very respectful memorial to Jim Thorpe can be found along PA 903, in what was once East Mauch Chunk.

Even in winter, downtown Jim Thorpe is alive with activity.

This group of homes on Race Street is called "Stone Row."

A block of coal, a railroad station turned visitor's center. What more could you want?

Sara Hayes and Earl Brown, of Dauphin County, enjoy their first trip to Jim Thorpe.

Just as they were in the 1800s, these gallows are in the old **CARBON COUNTY JAIL**, which was in use until 1995. This is the site of the famous "handprint on the wall" left by a Molly Maguire.

Space is tight downtown, so build it any way you can!

Early railroad developer Asa Packer lived in this handsome mansion overlooking the downtown.

Allan and Theresa Hayes, of Nash Creek, New Brunswick, with their daughter and son-in-law, Sara and Earl Brown, are also visiting Jim Thorpe for the first time. Here, they gaze at the amazing view from Penn's Peak, north of town.

Lehigh County

A truly beautiful county, Lehigh is dominated by the Allentown, Bethlehem, and Easton metro area, but there is much more to it. The covered bridge driving tour, for example, will give you a feel for the rural aspect of the county and a new appreciation for the diversity of the Lehigh Valley.

Hex signs! It must be Berks County! Well, almost. This one is in New Smithville, Lehigh County, just a bit east of the Berks County line.

It's not too often that you see a painted statue, like this one in Slatington, that honors firefighters.

Schnecksville, Lehigh County, is the site of **SCHLICHER'S COVERED BRIDGE**, unusual in that it dips slightly as you enter it.

Northampton County

In many ways like a twin to Lehigh County, Northampton County's big cities are Bethlehem and Easton. Bangor, in the north, is in the heart of the slate belt while Hellertown, in the south, is home to Lost River Caverns and the Goodman Campus of Lehigh University.

Not that I'm a fan of smoke, but there is an inherent beauty in many industrial sites, such as this cement plant in Bath, just one of many found throughout Northampton County.

Winter fun in Nazareth.

A great spring setting in Hellertown.

The headquarters of **MARTIN GUITARS**, respected around the world as makers of quality guitars, is right here in Nazareth.

The visitor center and museum at Martin's Guitars holds a wealth of exhibits, including these great custom guitars.

Bucks County

Really, Bucks County overwhelms the senses. So many outstanding places! From Doylestown, the county seat, to New Hope, Newtown, Bristol, and more than thirty miles of Delaware River shoreline; it is no exaggeration to say that this county comes as close to "having it all" as any county could.

The acclaimed **TOPEO GALLERY**, in New Hope, is one of the top galleries in the country for fine American crafts.

The **NEW HOPE AND IVYLAND RAILROAD** is a big tourist draw in very popular New Hope.

One of many old streets in New Hope.

A re-enactment of Washington crossing the Delaware, in, of all places, Washington Crossing, takes place on Christmas day.

Commemorating some really old places in Newtown.

Another one in Newtown, from the 1600s.

A perfect spring portrait of the **Newtown Friends Meeting House**.

As simple as it can be, there is as much purity and beauty in the meetinghouse
as there is in the most ornate building in the world.

This small sculpture in Newtown is a representation of the Peaceable Kingdom, an artistic concept by Edward Hicks, who lived nearby.

The **MERCER MUSEUM** in Doylestown is a treasure trove of artifacts of early American life.

Neither the time of the day nor the day of the week seems to matter...
Doylestown is always alive and thriving. It is also one beautiful community.

I actually thought the sign was more interesting
than the alley, so here's the sign.

Bristol, in southern Bucks County, takes advantage of its prime
location on the Delaware River.

Philadelphia

Philadelphia?! Well, it didn't seem fair to leave out one county, just because it's a big city. Like all big cities, Philadelphia has neighborhoods with a small town feel. These pictures are along Ridge Avenue in Roxborough, which is separated from most of the rest of the city by Fairmount Park. As for the turtle, it seems that the Wissahickon Creek watershed is a good breeding ground for turtles. That explanation sounded good to me, anyway.

Delaware County

Small, but densely populated: With industrial towns and heavily wooded residential areas, Delaware County is, to use the cliché, a study in contrasts. Plus, considering the way it comes together with Chester and Montgomery Counties, I don't know how anybody in that area ever figures out what county they're in. Bryn Mawr is in Montgomery County while nearby Villanova is in Delaware County and nearby Devon is in Chester County. Such is life in the suburbs, I guess! Delaware County is also the location of the first-rate Brandywine River Museum in Chadds Ford, the mention of which gives me the opportunity to include a great name for a town: Chadds Ford.

This SEPTA (Southeast Pennsylvania Transportation Authority) trolley in Media operates on the only remaining trolley line in the United States that runs right down a suburban street.

A pedestrian oasis in very busy downtown Media.

In Wallingford, this well-attended church strawberry festival provides lots of fun for all ages.

A mud run. Fun!

Samantha Tajirian and Steve Backall, both of nearby Springfield, do their part in the Mud Run, a fund-raiser for MS research, in Newtown Square.

Montgomery County

As I noted in the foreword, I didn't spend that much time on suburban areas. If I had done so, I could easily have filled a 200-page book with photos just of Montgomery County. Like all of the suburban Philadelphia counties, Montgomery County has mile after mile of beautiful residential communities: King of Prussia and Plymouth Meeting are two more names I wanted to be sure to include in this book!

GOLD MILLION RECORDS, located on Bryn Mawr's Main Line, houses some old records, yes, but also many, many items made from actual vinyl records! It's a must see for any music fan.

This is one of my favorite pictures. I thought that Moe Howard was no longer with us, but young Charles DiCanio has nailed the expression perfectly. Located in Ambler, Montgomery County, THE STOOGEUM houses a fantastic collection of "Three Stooges" memorabilia. If you're a Stooges fan, you'll love it; if not, well, that's okay, too.

Up the road, so to speak, in Montgomery County, is the Limerick nuclear power plant, whose plumes of water vapor are neatly silhouetted in the setting sun.

Mummers! Part of the St. Patrick's Day parade in Conshohocken, these are always one of the crowd pleasers. If you've never seen any of these groups in person, you can't appreciate how impressive they are.

Speaking of impressive, this downtown establishment in Conshohocken isn't bad, either.

This sculpture, on the campus of Ursinus College, is one of a number that can be found here and there, including the big one in Philadelphia.

Chester County

If you're not familiar with southeastern Pennsylvania and you come across some unfamiliar words, such as ones that have double consonants and internal "Ys" or "Ws" in odd places, then you're probably looking at a word with Welsh origins. Place names, such as Tredyffrin, Bala Cynwyd, Gwynedd, Bryn Mawr, and my favorite, Uwchlan, can be found in Chester and surrounding counties — and they are officially unpronounceable! Actually, there's a pronunciation guide at the end of the book, where I will try to iron it all out for you.

Kennett Square, Chester County, IS cool!

Kennett Square is also the mushroom capital of the world! There's a big festival celebrating that fact every September.

Kennett Square has one of the leafiest downtown streets of any place in this book. Here, the famous picture of Marilyn Monroe is re-created in this sculpture, placed out front of a downtown salon.

In nearby Avondale, the presence of the Latino community is evidenced by this display in front of a local market.

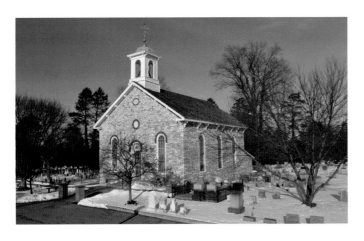

Situated along busy PA 252, this Baptist church in Great Valley, outside of Devon, really got my attention for its simple beauty.

This mural honors Harriet Tubman, who helped escaped slaves travel through the Underground Railroad.

Berks County

It was named for Berkshire, England, but it's clear that Berks is a county with a substantial German influence. Hex signs, horse and buggies, and, definitely, Pennsylvania Dutch being spoken here are all common sights and experiences in Berks County. Going beyond Reading in any direction, you'll find that the countryside quickly becomes mostly rural... It's a sightseer's and nature lover's dream.

The **DREIBELBIS COVERED BRIDGE**, near Lenhartsville, Berks County is also in on the hex sign tradition.

A barn/garage near Kutztown.

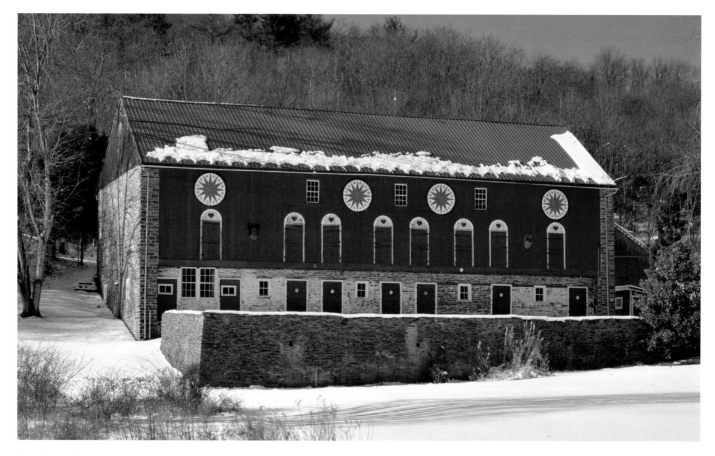

Another often photographed barn near Lenhartsville.

POP'S MALT SHOP in Kutztown, one of a relative few of its type that remain across the state.

Art in Boyertown... This one honors the local Pennsylvania Dutch heritage.

Who can argue with this advice?

In Hamburg, the King Frost parade is said to be the largest autumn parade in the East.

In Hamburg, after all, there must be a Hamburg-er Festival — and Jon Shuman, of **Spud's Restaurant** in Kutztown, helps to provide the "house specialty" during the festival.

Lebanon County

Geography suggests, accurately, as it turns out, that Lebanon County would be somewhat like Lancaster and Berks. It's true, and the Pennsylvania Dutch influence here is as strong as in either of those counties. In fact, you might hear one of the locals call it "LEP–nen" County! Having lived in the area for a few years, I was always struck by how consistently beautiful rural Lebanon County is.

This pedestrian bridge at **LEBANON VALLEY COLLEGE** (LVC) is quite the architectural statement.

Depending on your point of view, this shot, taken near Schaefferstown, is either a bleak scene or a beautiful late afternoon in winter. I'll choose the latter.

An old-time ice cream parlor remains in downtown Annville.

Black swans — another feature nearly unique to LVC.

Mt. Gretna is another one of those idyllic places that you might be afraid to believe can actually exist. The **HALL OF PHILOSOPHY** is just one of a group of architecturally uniform buildings in this heavily wooded community.

It seems like every street in Mt. Gretna provides another surprise.

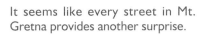

THE JIGGER SHOP, a venerable establishment in Mt. Gretna, is an old-time ice cream parlor that often has patrons standing in line ten deep to get their favorite dish.

This **SONIC**® in Palmyra just shouts out Americana.

Lancaster County

It's congested in some places, but Lancaster County is not overrated. It legitimately calls itself the "Garden Spot" for its superior farmland and picturesque villages. There are few other places in Pennsylvania where the terrain allows for miles-long vistas of farm after farm.

Ethan Lambert, of Mechanicsburg, is captivated by this railroad display in Strasburg.

Middlecreek Lake, in northern Lancaster County, is along the Atlantic Flyway. In March, thousands of snow geese rest here on their way northward.

Quilts like this one are prized items for visitors to Amish Country.

It doesn't happen every winter, but this one presented an opportunity for some outdoor ice hockey in Willow Street.

Kayleigh Deisey, of Lititz, enjoys the ducks at **LITITZ SPRINGS PARK**.

Even in outstanding Lancaster County, Lititz is a star.

Mark Shifflet, of Brunnerville, follows the tradition of rubbing the lion's nose for good luck. This sculpture, in **LITITZ SPRINGS PARK**, is modeled after a famous one in Lucerne, Switzerland.

Rolling through the scenic countryside of southern Lancaster County, the **STRASBURG RAILROAD** is always a picturesque site.

Here is the obligatory shot of an Amish farmer plowing his fields.

Nathan Lammey, working at one of the many Lancaster County establishments that cater to visitors who want to get a look at farm life, feels that "it provides opportunities for families to learn and play together while learning a little bit about agriculture."

Downtown Ephrata is a thriving and attractive community in northeastern Lancaster County.

I didn't ask the Channel 8 news crew what they were discussing, but apparently they were taking note of the fact that it was snowing in Manheim.

Sierra Miller, a student at **ELIZABETHTOWN COLLEGE**, gazes at the tranquility of the campus lake.

Street hockey, or rink hockey, in April, in Lampeter.

The riverfront in Columbia is a good place to watch the sunset over the broad Susquehanna River.

York County

Named for the English House of York, Pennsylvania's York County is vastly different from Lancaster County. It's much more hilly and somewhat within the sphere of influence of Baltimore, which is less than an hour away for many county residents.

The York County Heritage rail trail is one of the most diverse rail trails in the state. It offers some small towns, overpasses, woods, a tunnel, and it continues, if you dare to follow it, into Maryland. York County is also the location of sprawling Codorus State Park.

The surrounding communities are into this trail. At **GLATFELTERS STATION** is this tribute to bicyclists.

At **NEW FREEDOM**, these cyclists are headed back to their home in Maryland. The state line is less than a mile away.

A community with a name like Dillsburg *must* drop a pickle on New Year's Eve!

This mini park is in Dillsburg, northern York County, which is really considered part of the Harrisburg area.

Another sunset! This one is over Lake Marburg in **CODORUS STATE PARK**, near Hanover.

Adams County

Apples are a big commodity in Adams County, but any discussion of this county always comes back to Gettysburg. Let's not forget that Gettysburg was there before the battle... It's difficult to imagine what it must have been like for the townsfolk to have had such an enormous battle unfold right in front of them. Today the battlefield is maintained by the National Park Service and is visited by people from all over the world.

This recent addition to the Gettysburg streetscape is an interesting one. Abraham Lincoln, was not, after all, in Gettysburg to give directions, but the sculptures really are a plus for the town...

...but after seven months, the contemporary gentleman in the sweater still isn't getting it. (Couldn't resist that one.)

Near Carroll Valley, **SKI LIBERTY** attracts great crowds, many of whom are from the Baltimore-Washington area.

Bobbing for apples is part of the deal in this springtime ode to apples in Arendstville...

...and why not? After all, apples are a big deal in Adams County.

Anyone who can appreciate history cannot fail to be moved by the events of 1863 in Gettysburg. The battlefield is dotted with monuments from various states. This one, near the Pennsylvania monument, is stirring against the setting sun.

A nod to both the battle and the history of the Lincoln Highway, which runs right through Gettysburg.

This innovative way to display the red, white, and blue was seen along US 30 in Cashtown.

Franklin County

Named, of course, for Benjamin Franklin, Franklin County was the site of Civil War battles, including the burning of Chambersburg in 1864, that are lesser-known to the general public than Gettysburg. Along with Chambersburg, Waynesboro, Greencastle, Mercersburg, and a part of Shippensburg make up this border county that includes the major north-south route of Interstate 81.

Outside of Waynesboro... I just liked the colors in this scene.

On the east side of Waynesboro, Franklin County, this scene presented itself for a nice photo.

One of many tributes to the history of the Lincoln Highway, this one just west of Chambersburg.

Chambersburg peaches are every bit as prized as the ones from Georgia!

The apples in Chambersburg aren't bad either.

One of numerous, and very well done, Lincoln Highway commemorative murals, this one in St. Thomas.

Mercersburg means James Buchanan, and he's remembered in this downtown statue.

The town is also home to **MERCERSBURG ACADEMY**. These students are heading for the buses that will take them to their prom...in Baltimore!

Fulton County

Most of Fulton County lies between two ridges that separate it from Franklin and Bedford Counties. Some very steep grades leading into McConnellsburg were unavoidable for travelers on the old Lincoln Highway, but these have been replaced by a much improved US 30.

McConnellsburg on a late August evening.

In McConnellsburg, there is another in the series of Lincoln Highway murals, plus a highway marker like the one in Ligonier.

Bedford County

Bedford, situated as it is geographically, has been a hub of commerce since its beginnings. History abounds in this area, which includes Fort Bedford, Old Bedford Village, Bedford Springs, and, of course, the community of Bedford, so blessed with notable events and places that free walking tours are offered by the local chamber of commerce.

Everett weighs in with another first-rate mural.

Also along the Lincoln Highway were many examples of "kitsch" architecture. Some still survive, like this one in Bedford, although it's not in its original location.

Students at Bedford County Technical Center, acknowledging George Washington's role in the history of the area, built this giant quarter, which can be seen along US 30 between Bedford and Everett.

OLD BEDFORD VILLAGE frequently has programs celebrating the area's history.

This was a day commemorating the French and Indian War, which was big in these parts.

There is nothing, absolutely nothing, that is not first-class about the **BEDFORD SPRINGS RESORT AND SPA**. A few years ago, millions of dollars were poured into the resort, not just to restore it, but to make it better than it ever had been — and it's just as dazzling in the winter, maybe even more so.

One of the original Gulf gas stations still exists in Bedford. Gulf was an early leader in outstanding gas station architecture, including this Art Deco gem.

Built in 1828, the **BEDFORD COUNTY COURTHOUSE** is the oldest in continuous use in the state.

I will go out on a limb here and say that I doubt if Vincent Van Gogh was ever in Schellsburg, but of course, maybe I'm misinterpreting something. This is Vincent Van Gas, after all!

Dennis Tice, of the **BEDFORD AREA CHAMBER OF COMMERCE**, leads excellent free historical tours of downtown Bedford every Friday. This picture is a few years old, and I only mention that because the door on this building was replaced and that squeezed out George Washington's image, which is no longer there. He really did sleep here!

Most of US 30 still follows the route of the original Lincoln Highway. This scene is looking east, a few miles west of Bedford.

Blair County

Altoona is the big kahuna in this county, but Hollidaysburg and Tyrone, which, like Altoona, have strong connections to the railroad industry, each have a wealth of attractions worthy of your attention. In the mountainous region of this part of central Pennsylvania, Blair County will surprise at every turn. One minute, you're looking at a busy railroad yard, and the next, something akin to a "millionaire's row."

Here is the eastern entrance to Hollidaysburg, Blair County. Wouldn't you know that the Western Pennsylvania Conservancy changed all their signs shortly after I took this picture, but I decided to include it anyway!

Someone who should know gave me the inside scoop about this drawing on Allegheny Street in Hollidaysburg, apparently a touching tribute to the family pet. Trouble is, that isn't exactly what it's about. For me, however, it's going to remain a touching tribute to the family pet.

Canal Park memorializes Hollidaysburg's early history.

There it is... Home to one of the most famous toys in the world.

A pumpkin festival! Really, Hollidaysburg has it all.

This is one seriously large tree in Tyrone, a railroad town that takes pride in its heritage. My grandfather, a railroader, met my grandmother here.

GARDNER'S CANDIES, a beautiful and authentic old-time candy store, is located right in downtown Tyrone.

I guess we can't call it penny candy, but it's mighty close. Tuppence candy? If you have any appreciation for a store like this, which includes a small museum, then GARDNER'S CANDIES is a must see.

If you want a shot of a train coming around the bend as it passes by the Tyrone train station, you won't have to wait long. This is part of the old Pennsylvania Railroad main line, running from Philadelphia to Pittsburgh, and it's still heavily used by Norfolk Southern.

Good advice!

Clearfield County

To this eastern Pennsylvanian, Clearfield County always struck me as a transition zone between the state's east and west. As you head west on Interstate 80 from Milesburg, you begin a ten-mile climb up the Allegheny Front, finally reaching I-80's highest point east of the Mississippi, near mile marker 111.

The tranquil West Branch of the Susquehanna River as it flows through Clearfield.

Study this building in downtown Clearfield. The detail is amazing.

This plot of land outside of town is tended to by a very generous individual. Unfortunately, one of the bears is missing.

Clearfield is the only community in Pennsylvania that lies on both sides of the Susquehanna, so the river is never very far away.

MCGEES MILLS COVERED BRIDGE is the only remaining covered bridge in Clearfield County, and the only remaining one over the Susquehanna.

Brandon Shaw and Dakota, just after Dakota won the best costumed pet contest during the Relay for Life events in DuBois. Brandon explained that Dakota's wings represented a guardian angel to look over all patients battling cancer.

Clinton County

Hang gliding near Renovo, summer concerts, the West Branch, and Lock Haven… I particularly admire Lock Haven. Devastated by numerous floods, abandoned over the years by some major industries, Lock Haven doesn't look like a town that's down and out — and that's because it isn't! With a beautiful setting, a cool downtown, and a great college atmosphere, this city radiates pride and optimism.

Here's a nice gas station near Mill Hall, in Clinton County, except it isn't a gas station. It's actually a car dealership, absolutely full of gas station memorabilia.

Richard Bowman has spent more than thirty years collecting these items. He could open this up as a museum and charge admission… It's that good.

Lock Haven

Due to numerous devastating floods over the years, Lock Haven gave up its spectacular riverfront view to save the city and the result was superb. Continuously used by walkers and joggers, the view can still be enjoyed by those who take advantage of the path along the top of the flood protection earthen wall.

Nice purple flower, only it's an invasive species called purple loosestrife, blooming in profusion along the West Branch of the Susquehanna in Lock Haven, Clinton County.

Lock Haven remains an impressive community, with many fine homes, made all the more spectacular by a November snow squall.

On Sunday nights in the summer, the waterfront plays host to concerts, thanks to the amphitheater that was built as part of the flood control project. The enduring group Hybrid Ice plays to a nice crowd on this sultry night in July.

Centre County

I love State College, but Centre County isn't all about State College. Bellefonte could hold its own here — and does. It's a long way from Philipsburg to Millheim, but they, too, are part of Centre County, geographically the second largest in the state. Boalsburg, fiercely claiming to be the true birthplace of Memorial Day, is also part of this county.

This is only three-sevenths of it. There are four more governors on the other side. Bellefonte, in Centre County, was home to no less than seven governors, most from Pennsylvania.

Daffodils abound by the thousands in April. They've become a signature of Bellefonte and can be found all over town, especially in and around TALLEYRAND PARK.

Daffodils grow in profusion on the banks of **SPRING CREEK** while Palomino
trout share the creek with ducklings. Neither seems to mind the other.

The number of massive buildings in downtown Bellefonte is impressive in itself.

You know the food is fresh!

From the steps of the **CENTRE COUNTY COURTHOUSE**, you get a look at still another grand old downtown building — the **BROCKERHOFF HOUSE**.

Memorial Day in Boalsburg

Although other towns lay claim to the title, Boalsburg, just east of State College, is insistent that it is the birthplace of Memorial Day — and it honors that tradition every year with an elaborate ceremony.

Around 6:00 p.m., the ceremonies are solemn and respectful.

Period dress is part of the ceremony.

This mural celebrates the heritage of Millheim, in eastern Centre County.

At the opposite end of sprawling Centre County is Philipsburg, actually closer in spirit to Clearfield County.

Just a bit farther east of Boalsburg, on US 322, is a Harley-Davidson outlet, featuring this eye-catching horse made from the discarded chrome of old Harleys.

Huntingdon County

Another county which can vary dramatically from place to place. This is the site of Raystown Lake, a Mecca for boating and fishing, and highly scenic as well. The county is also the location of Shaver's Creek Environmental Center, a venture of Penn State that conducts environmental education programs for children and adults alike.

At Mayfest, which is, of course, held in April, Lynda Kuckenbrod demonstrates her skills as a clinical harpist. Playing in nursing homes and hospitals, Lynda provides a comforting lift to those whose spirits need lifting. In her own words, she is a "sound therapist." Think about that. It works!

Another one of those "coolest towns" is Huntingdon. This quiet scene is right downtown.

Part of a large wall design, this mosaic is a bona fide work of art.

A college campus with hardly anyone out and about. It might have something to do with the fact that it was 15 degrees on the day of this picture!

JUNIATA COLLEGE is one of the reasons Huntingdon is a "cool town!"

Mifflin County

Long and stretched out (geographically speaking), Mifflin County includes Lewistown, Burnham, Yeagertown, Reedsville, Milroy, and, one of my favorite words, the Kishacoquillas Valley. The county's proximity to State College and its rugged mountain scenery make it a desirable, lower cost alternative to living across the mountain in so-called Happy Valley.

You may assume that this little hamlet in the Kishacoquillas Valley is Pennsylvania Dutch Country ...

... but many people don't realize that there are Amish folks living in many parts of Pennsylvania, other than Lancaster County. A trip to the store, while the horse waits patiently, is a typical scene, like this one near Belleville.

I wouldn't normally cut off a statue like this, but it works, I think, for this shot of downtown Lewistown.

THE WATERFRONT TAVERN in Lewistown provides a relaxing outdoor setting, with a view of the Juniata River. I never like to ask people at a meal if they would mind having their picture taken, but these two were fine with it — they work here!

Juniata County

Like a twin to Mifflin County, but without as much industry, Juniata County is actually one of the most rural counties in the central to southeastern part of the state. And like Mifflin County, Juniata follows the contours of two very long mountain ridges, with most of its land area between them.

For a small county, the **JUNIATA COUNTY COURTHOUSE** in Mifflintown is an imposing structure.

This view of Mifflintown from **JUNIATA HIGH SCHOOL** shows just how mountainous this region is.

Perry County

The part of Perry County that borders the Susquehanna River can be a sometimes hectic place, but go a few miles away from there and you're in a different world. New Bloomfield, the county seat, is as tranquil as county seats get, and most of the rest of farmed and forested Perry County is just as good.

It would seem that this is just a traffic light, but this is no ordinary traffic light. Well, actually, it is, but its significance is that it's the only one in Perry County. The light is a recent addition because of busy, and often heavily congested, US 11 and 15. Forest County is now the only county without a working traffic light.

New Bloomfield, the seat of Perry County, is home to the **CARSON LONG MILITARY ACADEMY**.

The Statue of Liberty pops up sometimes in the most unexpected places. This is a fine representation in Millerstown.

A perfect October day at Carson Long.

Cumberland County

The beautiful Cumberland Valley includes Shippensburg, Newville, Big Spring, and the west shore communities of the Harrisburg area. Carlisle is home to some big time car shows, the Army War College, and the Army Heritage Center. If that isn't enough history, Jim Thorpe attended the former Carlisle Indian School, and the old courthouse in Carlisle still shows some scars from Civil War shelling.

Shippensburg, mostly in Cumberland County, partly in Franklin County, is the site of this corn-eating contest in September.

Built in 1798, the **McLean House** is now a Bed and Breakfast.

Shippensburg University is the site of the state track and field championships held in late May.

Swans, a lake, and a town called Boiling Springs. Does it get any better?

Gary King, of Mechanicsburg, plays along for the camera as he demonstrates his ability to ring the little kids bell with ease at Mechanicsburg's annual Jubilee Day™.

In Mechanicsburg, stalactites can become stalagmites, that is, if you break off icicles and "plant" them upside down. Rather artistic, really.

Dauphin County

Dauphin County is, of course, the location of our state capital. From Middletown in the south to the northern communities of Millersburg, Halifax, and Elizabethville, and also to Hershey and Hummelstown, Dauphin County is another one of those counties that could easily generate a thick volume to describe it.

The nature and arts festival, a program sponsored by the **NED SMITH CENTER FOR NATURE AND ART**, is held in late July in Millersburg. Jut McDaniels, of Shaver's Creek Environmental Center, near State College, demonstrates his skills with a black snake to an attentive visitor.

The **NED SMITH CENTER FOR NATURE AND ART**, near Millersburg, sponsors programs about nature, art, and conservation. This first-class facility is an asset to Millersburg and northern Dauphin County that other places can only dream about.

As part of its bicentennial celebration in 2007, Millersburg sponsored a bench painting contest. This one ended up in front of a local downtown bank.

Downtown Millersburg looks like it's right out of a book of Americana.

The pedestrian bridge over Wiconisco Creek provides a great view of the mile-wide Susquehanna River.

This circular radiator was a unique feature of the old 5 and 10, which is now closed.

The Millersburg ferry is the only ferry boat still crossing the Susquehanna River.

Don Lebo has piloted the *Roaring Bull* for twenty-two years.

The paddle wheel is for real!

This grove of sycamores accents PA 147, just south of Halifax.

Justin Chortanoff, of Steelton, poses with an art object originally in Harrisburg. He'll match the art on his right arm, square inch for square inch, with the cow!

This is only a small part of a roadside stand along PA 225 in Halifax. The fall display is so impressive that it's worth driving for miles just to see it.

The Star Barn is a Middletown landmark, although it's slated to be moved to a proposed agricultural heritage center in Lebanon County. The real story here, however, is with the individuals in the picture. Leisa Dupes suffered from kidney failure and needed a transplant. Her husband Mike, left, was a high school classmate and longtime friend of Jan-Michael Lawrence, seen here on the right. In an extraordinary act of friendship and generosity, Jan-Michael donated a kidney to Leisa, and the transplant was successful. The symbolism here is pure poetry.

Middletown, the oldest town in Dauphin County, is one of the most close-knit communities in the Harrisburg area.

Elijah Flasher, Anthony Chambers, and Anthony DuBois, of Middletown Area High School's Class of 2011, get ready to attend their graduation ceremony at the Forum in Harrisburg.

Meanwhile, Melissa Hare is all smiles as she poses with her family at the same graduation.

THE SODA JERK, in Hummelstown, is another one of those retro ice cream parlor/diners that can still be found if you're looking.

Downtown Hummelstown's makeover includes a prominent reference to nearby Indian Echo Caverns.

It's after closing time, but people usually aren't in a hurry to leave!

Schuylkill County

The northern part of Schuylkill County is in the heart of the southern anthracite region. Ashland, Mahanoy City, Girardville, Shenandoah, Minersville, and St. Clair were all centers of active mining. Today, mining remains an important industry, but the massive banks of coal waste left behind are now being used to fuel cogeneration plants. The purpose of this industry is to produce electricity using waste from days gone by, and to use the remaining ash byproduct to fill in the abandoned strip pits. Sometimes there is such a thing as a win-win situation!

Shamokin and surrounding Coal Township are in Northumberland County, but are really the gateway, at least to the southern anthracite coal region.

Sarah Dagostin and Charlene Hook actually agreed to willingly pose in front of four tons of coal in Ashland, Schuylkill County.

In the heart of coal country is Shenandoah's elaborate miner's memorial.

On a hill overlooking PA 61 in Ashland is this likeness of the famous Whistler's Mother portrait.

Notice the miner's cap light in this unique memorial near Minersville.

Tamaqua is definitely not in western Pennsylvania, but the Western Pennsylvania Conservancy had a hand in developing this plot downtown.

Another bunch of critters look for a handout in Schuylkill Haven.

Nice job. Very nice job on Tamaqua's downtown park.

That's a "flatiron building" in the background. There are more of them around than one might suspect.

Local "isms" on display at the history center in Tamaqua.

Northumberland County

It may be the most oddly shaped county in the state, primarily because, in the post-Revolutionary era, pieces of it were continually carved away to form other counties. From Shamokin and Mt. Carmel in the east, to Sunbury, Northumberland, and Herndon in the west, and Milton and Watsontown in the north, the county has very distinct parts. In Sunbury, you'll find the world's longest inflatable dam, first electric light (sort of), smallest restaurant (at least there can't be very many that are smaller), and a street grid named after the streets of early Philadelphia, which most local residents aren't even aware of.

The **SUSQUEHANNA UNIVERSITY** women's crew team practices on the Susquehanna near Sunbury.

Connecting Northumberland and Snyder counties, this is the world's longest inflatable dam. When it was built in the 1960s, it had some problems, but since then, it has created a pool deep enough for boating in the otherwise too shallow Susquehanna River.

Charlie and Nicco Dalpiaz get their first up-close look at the restored fountain after its return to **CAMERON PARK**. A nod goes to my cousin, Tom Wolfe, who spent countless hours restoring it to working order after it was neglected in storage for decades.

A disastrous flood prompted the building of the flood protection wall, sealing off the view of the mighty Susquehanna from Front Street in Sunbury, but views like this one are still accessible.

A Sunbury landmark since 1945, the **SQUEEZE INN**, built between two downtown buildings, is a whopping seven feet wide! DaVina Young and regular customer Doug Getgen successfully play living statues for this time exposure.

Trains that come right up along Third Street are an everyday occurrence.

When one flag isn't enough, decorate the street sign pole!

Not many people outside the Sunbury area know about Thomas Edison's connection to the city, but, in 1883, he supervised the wiring of the City Hotel on this site, making it the first electrically wired hotel in the world.

KEITHAN'S BLUE BIRD GARDENS, found at the south end of Sunbury, is a paradise for those who love spring blooming shrubs and trees, such as dogwood, azaleas, and rhododendrons.

Although Northumberland and Sunbury are part of the same school district, the North Branch of the Susquehanna does sort of set off one part of Northumberland County from the other. If you know what a Pineknotter is, then you probably know something about Northumberland. It has much more of a history than a casual observer might suspect. Joseph Priestley, one of the world's renowned scientists, chose to leave England in 1794 for religious reasons, and built the home that remains today along the banks of the North Branch. And any town with street names like "Duke, Queen, King, Orange, Hanover, and Prince" just might have some English heritage. And that Pineknotter? The name comes from the logs that were floated down the waters of the West Branch. The former Northumberland High School's athletic teams were called the "Pineknotters."

Right in Northumberland, **Weaver Models** makes fine custom model railroad cars with care and precision.

Also in Northumberland is **Resilite**, manufacturer of about 75% of all wrestling mats and related products used in high schools and colleges throughout the country. Long ago, I witnessed someone dropping a raw egg on one of these mats to demonstrate that the egg wouldn't break. It didn't.

Don't have a pool? No problem, just do it the old-fashioned way by taking advantage of the West Branch of the Susquehanna, in Northumberland.

The West Branch of the Susquehanna can provide some spectacular summertime sunsets.

In northern Northumberland County, Milton was, and still is, the industrial giant of the region. **ACF INDUSTRIES**, one of my former employers, was the builder of the first railroad tank car, seen here in this replica.

Downtown Milton has undertaken some major improvement projects, including three first-rate murals. This is part of the most recent one.

This was the first one, depicting Milton's considerable heritage.

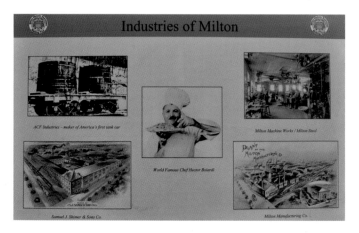

An extensive walking tour provides insights into Milton's past and present.

Montour County

Tiny Montour County's hub is Danville. Once home to several major industries, Danville still can point to the behemoth Geisinger Medical Center as its major employer.

An interesting tradition. Danville prom-goers leave their cars, and their keys, to walk down Mill Street, greeting friends and family on their way to the prom.

Immaculately maintained **ZAMBONI PARK** in Danville overlooks the North Branch of the Susquehanna.

An early morning mist accentuates the attributes of this park near the Danville-Riverside Bridge.

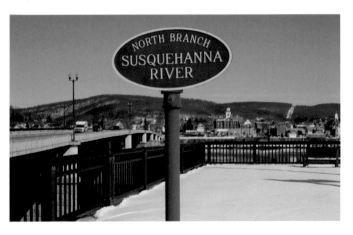

A view from Riverside overlooks the bridge to Danville.

At **LIBERTY VALLEY ELEMENTARY**, outside Danville, these autumn figures stand in slightly scary repose against the late evening sky.

In order to minimize damage to Danville's historic district, the realignment of PA 54 employed a "cut and cover" process (a tunnel).

Yes, it's big enough to need a shuttle from the parking lot. **GEISINGER MEDICAL CENTER** dominates the landscape in and around Danville, and it just keeps growing.

Columbia County

Columbia County is radically different from north to south. Northern Columbia County is heavily forested while the southern tip of the county is part of the coal region. In between are the small "urban" hubs of Bloomsburg and Berwick.

Dennis Eisenhauer, Nate Blass, Zac Appleman, and Jeff Knorr all hang out at the fountain for this photo shoot. Although this shot took place on April 30th, a threat of frost the night before resulted in turning off the water.

Bloomsburg, the county seat, has a most impressive town fountain. Note that the water goes *into*, not out from, the fountain.

Low lying parts of Bloomsburg are flood prone, but the misty morning view of the usually placid Susquehanna is spectacular.

In southern Columbia County lies what's left of Centralia. A few houses still remain, but the underground coal mine fire has been burning for nearly fifty years and the state has relocated most residents. Ironically, a future energy source can be seen in the distance.

Built by the Boy Scouts of America in the 1950s, this "Little Sister of Liberty," in Berwick, is one of only three remaining in Pennsylvania. The others are in nearby Bloomsburg and in Elwood City.

Taylor and Tristian Farr demonstrate their skateboarding skills at an undisclosed location in Berwick. I'll take responsibility for the "undisclosed location" part, because I seriously didn't notice the very prominently displayed "No Skateboarding" sign until this short photo shoot was almost over!

How can you not like a field of pumpkins? They're almost as showy as sunflowers, as this field near Berwick confirms.

Another scene outside of Berwick...on a road I'm not sure I could find again if my life depended on it.

Just like the sign says in the tiny hamlet of Central, northern Columbia County is the gateway to the gamelands.

Sullivan County

It's like everybody's favorite county. With one of the state's smallest populations, Sullivan County is mostly about woods, game lands, overlooks, covered bridges, and consciously quaint little towns.

There is just something about the **SONESTOWN INN** in Sullivan County that I find to be very appealing.

Sitting high in the Endless Mountains is Eagles Mere, kind of a dream of a town that takes you back one hundred years. Sort of a Mt. Gretna for mountain types.

One very present day activity, though, is the toboggan run, built by local volunteers, and enjoyed by people of all ages from around the region and beyond.

The Native American Pow Wow, held in Forksville, is an educational experience for participants and spectators alike.

The berries of this Washington Hawthorn provide great color to a winter day in Laporte, with the **SULLIVAN COUNTY COURTHOUSE** in the background.

Spanning Loyalsock Creek, the **FORKSVILLE COVERED BRIDGE**, unlike some that have been converted to tourist attractions, is in constant use.

I won't try to explain this one in Dushore, Sullivan County. It's called an outhouse race. They race mobile "outhouses." Neat, though!

Lycoming County

It's the largest county in the state and it seems that way. From Jersey Shore in the west, to Hughesville in the east, and from Allenwood in the south, almost to Liberty in the north, Lycoming County covers about 1,200 square miles, making it slightly larger than Rhode Island. It straddles the geologic valley and ridge province in the south, and the Allegheny plateau in the north.

Small town, big old handsome homes: Muncy, in eastern Lycoming County, is loaded with them.

A perfect day and hot air balloons. How can you go wrong? This event, sponsored by Lycoming County rotary clubs, was held in Montoursville, but has been moved to Hughesville to get away from river fog.

Jersey Shore is supposedly so named because some early residents were from New Jersey, and were referred to by people across the river as those on the "Jersey shore."

The "Fanny" float down the West Branch between Jersey Shore and Williamsport has been revived, shown here at Linden. As you can tell from the picture, participation was outstanding.

The Little League World Series

The Little League World Series in South Williamsport is an experience. First-time visitors are overwhelmed by the fact that it really is a world series and many players and their families are here from the far corners of the earth.

The championship game usually draws a full house, including the thousands sitting on the bank beyond the outfield.

Colton Harer and Tony Gordon, from nearby Montgomery, are fully into the scene.

This crew from Edogawa Minami Little League, Tokyo, is having the time of their lives.

Just a few miles south of Williamsport, on US 15, Frank Payne, of Reptiland, carefully feeds one of the specialty zoo's alligators. **REPTILAND** also includes a new exhibit on dinosaurs that will blow you away!

Just a bit farther south on Route 15 is another one of my favorite retro style places. **WEAVER'S RESTAURANT**, in Allenwood, Union County, should be a mandatory stop for anyone who enjoys seeing memorabilia of this type.

Union County

Union County isn't that big, but there is a good deal going on here. Between Mifflinburg and Lewisburg, it seems that one or the other is always hosting some special event. Home to Bucknell University, Lewisburg is one of those places that sometimes seems too good to be true. If you think there's no social or cultural life in a small town, try Lewisburg. Mifflinburg, though university-less, is also the epitome of small town charm. There can't be many towns its size that know how to put on special events the way Mifflinburg does.

Referring to Mifflinburg's skills at putting on festivals, shown here is Christkindl, a December street festival featuring traditions with a German theme. It is first-rate in every way.

Just as with the pumpkins, but this time they're sunflowers, how can you not love a field of them? This photogenic plot was east of Mifflinburg.

It's thriving, and it's just plain cool. Lewisburg is full of unique businesses, and is heavily influenced by the presence of Bucknell University.

This is also the buggy exit ...

... and speaking of that, Mifflinburg was home to a buggy making industry, and has a museum to document its history.

The Lewisburg polar bear plunge... I don't know how they do it! I really don't.

A late fall and an early snow combine to produce this unusual shot.

Barnes and Noble has partnered with Bucknell to bring one of its bookstores to downtown Lewisburg. On a cold winter night, that bookstore looks very inviting.

The annual Independence Day celebration is one of Lewisburg's major events, and is actually held a week early.

You could write a reasonably sized book about Third Street alone.

From this still picture, we'll never know for sure if his foot really was on the line, but in this game with Lafayette, the Bucknell Bison prevailed at the majestic Sojka pavilion.

Snyder County

Snyder County is named for Pennsylvania's only three-term governor, Selinsgrove resident Simon Snyder. Mostly rural, the county nonetheless includes the largest retail area between Harrisburg and Williamsport. Home to highly regarded Susquehanna University, Selinsgrove has been described as "nicely understated" according to the local newspaper. There's no lack of activity here, unless you're accustomed to living in Manhattan.

It may be bear country ahead, but I wouldn't mess with that guy over there by the fence, either. **T AND D'S CATS OF THE WORLD**, near Penns Creek, Snyder County, is a sanctuary for more than just cats, although there are plenty of them to be seen, too.

It might seem fortunate that I caught these ducks in flight in Middleburg, but I'm the one who unintentionally scared them away.

SELINSGROVE AREA HIGH SCHOOL is just one part of the school district campus.

Dating back to veterans of the Civil War, the **McClure Bean Soup** is an annual event held in this western Snyder County community. The tasty dish is traditionally made with beef, not ham.

A former bank has become a new restaurant downtown.

Trevor Kerstetter and Chad Drzewiecki discuss Life, the Universe, and Everything, or something like that, in front of the **Kind Café**, another popular downtown spot.

A full house attends Susquehanna University's Christmas Candlelight Service in **Weber Chapel Auditorium**.

River towns have river views, and Selinsgrove is no exception. At the home of his grandparents, Grady Dionne checks out the garden railroad.

Taken just a few hundred feet from the previous picture, and obviously on a different day, this shot of the Susquehanna River is a reminder of why small town life can be very, very satisfying.

Pronunciation Guide

Arendtsville: "Arendts" ryhmes with "Warrants"
Bala Cynwyd: BAL (rhymes with pal) – uh – KIN – wid
Charleroi: SHAR – luh – roi
Codorus: kuh – DOR – is
Conneaut: CONN – ay – ott
Kishacoquillas: KISH – uh – co – QUILL – us
Lancaster: LANK – is – ter
Medix Run: MEED – ix (so I'm told)
Lycoming: Local residents say "lie – KUMM – ing," everybody else says "lie – KOME – ing"
Ohiopyle: Ohio + pile
Renovo: reh – NO – vuh
Schuylkill: SKOOK – uhl, or SKUHLK – uhl, or if you're not hip, SCHOOL – KILL
Selinsgrove: SEAL – ins – grove (the middle syllable is INS, not INGS)
Shamokin: sha – MO – kin
Tamaqua: tuh – MOCK – wuh
Tredyffrin: truh – DIFF – rin
Tunkhannock: tunk – HANN – uck
Uwchlan: YEW – klin (Closer to the original Welsh is ESH – lon)

EMMA'S FOOD FOR LIFE features a unique menu, using locally raised products.

Index